New Classics to Moderns

6

Contents

Yorktown Music Press

Les Triolets

from Nouvelles Suites de Pièces de Clavecin

Jean-Philippe Rameau
1683–1764

© Copyright 2014 Yorktown Music Press.
All Rights Reserved. International Copyright Secured.

Petite Reprise

Prelude No.19 in A Major

from The Well-Tempered Clavier, Book I

Johann Sebastian Bach
1685–1750

© Copyright 2014 Yorktown Music Press.
All Rights Reserved. International Copyright Secured.

Andante

2nd Movement *from* Overture No.1, Op.1

Carl Friedrich Abel
1723–1787

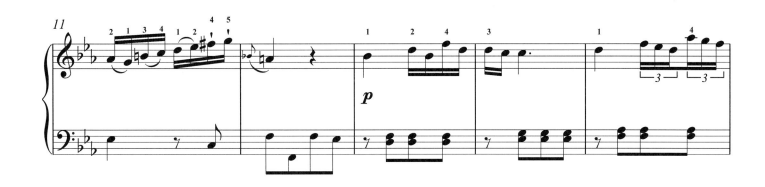

© Copyright 2014 Yorktown Music Press.
All Rights Reserved. International Copyright Secured.

Minuet No.3

from 12 Minuets, Hob.IX:11

Joseph Haydn
1732–1809

MINUET
Allegro con brio

Fine

© Copyright 2014 Yorktown Music Press.
All Rights Reserved. International Copyright Secured.

Minuet D.C. al Fine

Rondo in A Major

WoO.49

Ludwig van Beethoven
1770–1827

© Copyright 2014 Yorktown Music Press.
All Rights Reserved. International Copyright Secured.

Cantabile in B♭ Major

B.84

Frédéric Chopin
1810–1849

© Copyright 2014 Yorktown Music Press.
All Rights Reserved. International Copyright Secured.

Mazurka in C Major, Op.7 No.5

Frédéric Chopin
1810–1849

Dal Segno 𝄋 senza Fine

© Copyright 2014 Yorktown Music Press.
All Rights Reserved. International Copyright Secured.

At An Old Trysting Place

No.3 *from* 10 Woodland Sketches, Op.51

Edward Macdowell
1860–1908

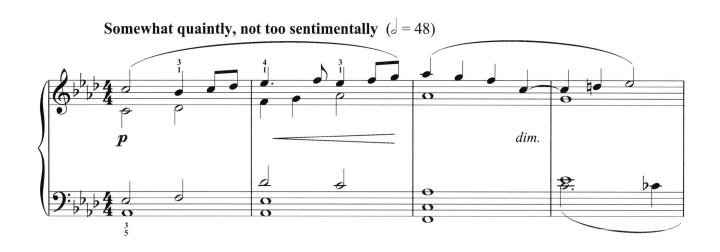

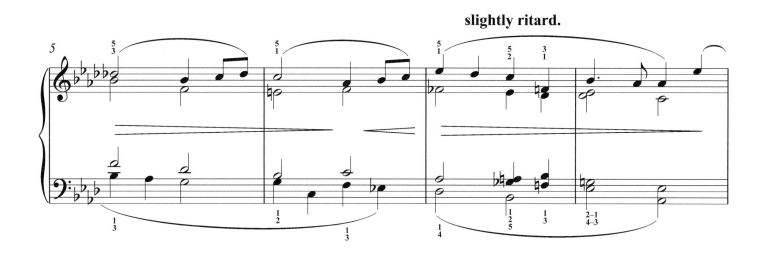

© Copyright 2014 Yorktown Music Press.
All Rights Reserved. International Copyright Secured.

Française d'après Claude Gervaise

Francis Poulenc
1899–1963

© Copyright 1940 Novello & Company Limited.
All Rights Reserved. International Copyright Secured.

Allegro

No. 5 *from* Five Short Pieces

Lennox Berkeley
1903–1989

© Copyright 1937 Chester Music Limited.
All Rights Reserved. International Copyright Secured.

The Schoolmaster

from Folk Melodies

Witold Lutoslawski
1913–1994

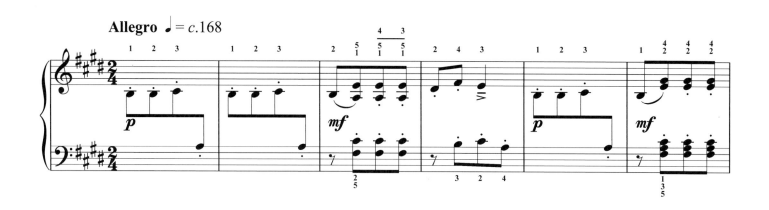

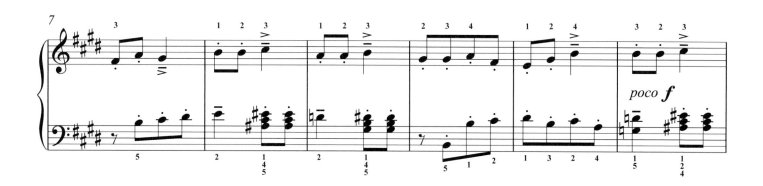

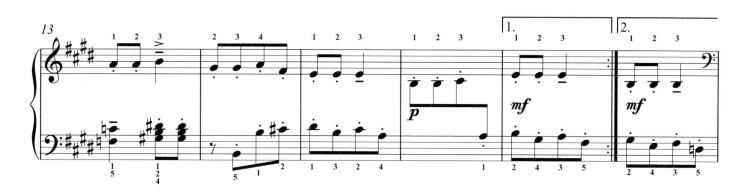

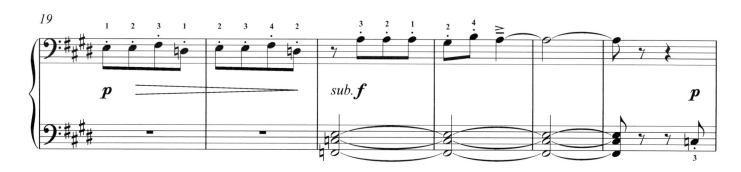

© Copyright 1947 Polskie Wydawnictwo Muzyczne - PWM Edition, Krakow. Copyright renewed 1975 by Polskie Wydawnictwo Muzyczne - PWM Edition.
Exclusively Licensed to Chester Music Limited in 1990 for the World except Albania, Bosnia and Herzegovina, Bulgaria, China, Croatia, Cuba, Czech Republic, Estonia, Hungary, Latvia, Lithuania,
Macedonia, North Korea, Poland, Romania, Russian Federation, Serbia and Montenegro, Slovakia, Slovenia, Ukraine, Vietnam and the Commonwealth of Independent States (CIS).
All Rights Reserved. International Copyright Secured.

Eight Maids a-Milking

from Partridge Pie

Richard Rodney Bennett
1936–2012

con poco di ped.

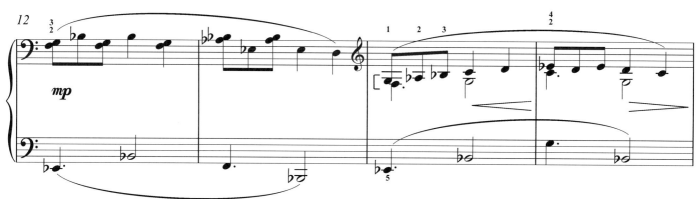

© Copyright 1991 Novello & Company Limited.
All Rights Reserved. International Copyright Secured.

Elegía A Maurice Ravel

Xavier Montsalvatge
1912–2002

© Copyright Union Musical Ediciones, S.L. Madrid (España).
Chester Music Limited.
All Rights Reserved. International Copyright Secured.

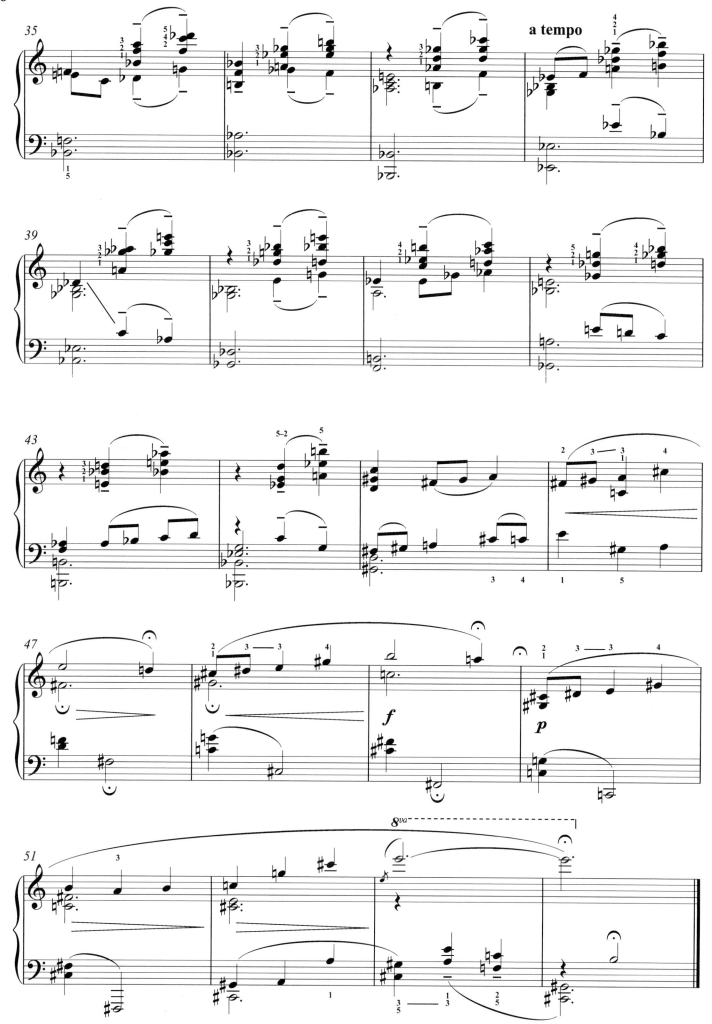

L'Origine Nascosta

Ludovico Einaudi
b.1955

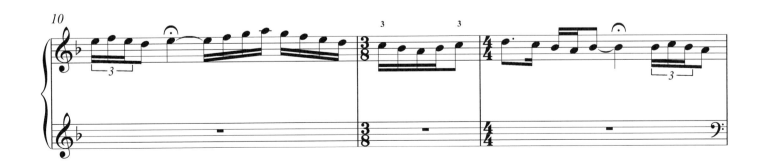

© Copyright 2006 Chester Music Limited.
All Rights Reserved. International Copyright Secured.

Published by
Wise Music Group
14-15 Berners Street,
London W1T 3LJ, UK.

Exclusive Distributors:
Hal Leonard
7777 West Bluemound Road,
Milwaukee, WI 53213
Email: info@halleonard.com

Hal Leonard Europe Limited
42 Wigmore Street, Marylebone,
London WIU 2 RY
Email: info@halleonardeurope.com

Hal Leonard Australia Pty. Ltd.
4 Lentara Court, Cheltenham,
Victoria 9132, Australia
Email: info@halleonard.com.au

Order No. YK22165
ISBN 978-1-78305-376-6

This book © Copyright 2014 Yorktown Music Press,
a part of Wise Music Group.

For all works contained herein:
Unauthorized copying, arranging, adapting, recording, Internet posting,
public performance, or other distribution of the music in this publication
is an infringement of copyright. Infringers are liable under the law.

Edited by Sam Lung.
Music processing and layout by Camden Music Services.

Printed in the EU.

www.halleonard.com